RED-HOT BIKES
TRIUMPH

Daniel Gilpin

W
FRANKLIN WATTS
LONDON•SYDNEY

First published in 2007 by
Franklin Watts
338 Euston Road
London NW1 3BH

Franklin Watts Australia
Level 17/207 Kent Street
Sydney NSW 2000

Series editor: Adrian Cole
Series design: Big Blu
Art director: Jonathan Hair

A CIP catalogue record for this book is available from the British Library.

ISBN: 978 0 7496 7148 8

Dewey Classification: 629.227'5

Acknowledgements:
The Publisher would like to thank Triumph.
All images © Triumph 2007

Every attempt has been made to clear copyright. Should there be any
inadvertent omission please apply to the publisher for rectification.

Printed in China

Franklin Watts is a division of Hachette Children's Books.

Contents

Triumph – go your own way

Triumph has been making motorbikes for more than 100 years. The company was founded and is still based in England. Today it is the country's biggest motorbike manufacturer, employing more than 1,000 people worldwide. The company motto is 'Go your own way'.

Proud history

Triumph bikes are designed and built at the company's state-of-the-art production plant in Hinckley, Leicestershire. As a company, Triumph has a long and proud history. It produced motorbikes for the British Army in both World War I and World War II (1914–18 and 1939–45). During peacetime, it created models that went on to become classics. Those early models continue to inspire the Triumph bikes built today.

Tech talk

Employing – when a company gives people jobs.

Manufacturer – a person or company that makes things.

Naked – a class of motorbike that has very few body panels (fairings).

↑ The Triumph factory at Hinckley is one of the last remaining bike production plants in Britain.

Full throttle facts

Company name: Triumph Motorcycles Ltd
Year of founding: 1887
First bike model: No.1 (launched in 1902)

Employees: 1,000 worldwide (600 in the UK)
Headquarters: Hinckley, UK
President: Privately owned by Mr John Bloor

Best of British

Triumph is a company that is proud to be British. The bikes it makes are the product of years of research and development. They have a unique character that sets them apart from anything else on the road. Triumph makes a wide range of bike models. The six models featured in this book include the powerful, naked Triumph Speed Triple and the modern, lightweight Daytona 675. All the bikes are produced for a great riding experience, one of the company's founding aims.

⬆ From left to right: the Triumph Speed Triple, Daytona 675 and Sprint ST are three of the six models featured in this book.

Number of bikes sold: 40,000 per year
Number of models: 12

Best-selling model: Speed Triple
Manufacturing plants: 2

5

Triumph Speed Triple

The Speed Triple is a bike that screams power. It has a tough aluminium chassis that carries a potent 1050 cc, in-line 3-cylinder engine. The Speed Triple is named after this engine.

Naked style

The Speed Triple's styling is raw and aggressive, and is inspired by the 'naked' look popular in Europe. The short, stubby twin exhausts produce a sound like an angry beast, and give the bike a tough character all of its own. The tail is short and angled upwards and is part of the characteristic look of the Speed Triple.

⬆ The Speed Triple is a street machine with attitude. Its styling has been designed to appeal to younger riders. This model is fitted with modified Arrow exhausts that are mounted lower down on the bike.

Full throttle facts

Top speed: 220 kph
Length: 2,115 mm

Handlebar width: 780 mm
Fuel capacity: 18 litres

3-cylinder engine

The 3-cylinder engine layout is almost a Triumph trademark. Over the years it has featured in most of their bikes. The Speed Triple celebrates this fact both in its name and its design, with the engine shown off more clearly than in any other Triumph bike. Even the exhaust is wrapped beneath the engine to prevent the pipes from covering anything up.

⬆ *The twin headlights are a distinctive feature of the Speed Triple, as are the upside down front forks.*

Tech talk

Exhaust – the pipes through which the gas emissions from an engine are expelled.

Front forks – the telescopic, spring-loaded units that connect the front wheel to the rest of the bike.

In-line – refers to the placement of the engine cylinders in a row.

Styling – when something is shaped and made in a particular way.

Kerb weight: 189 kg
Seat height: 815 mm

Engine capacity: 1050 cc
Gearbox: 6-speed

Top performer

The Speed Triple was first introduced by Triumph in 1994 – it was an instant hit with riders. Many people like its naked street styling, speed and high performance levels. The 1050 cc engine delivers a massive amount of power, and because the bike has a lightweight aluminium frame, it can accelerate quickly. The bike is also easy to manoeuvre and control at high speed.

Triumph Speed Triple

Short, stumpy exhausts

Lightweight aluminium chassis

Front suspension

Single-sided swingarm

Liquid-cooled, in-line 3-cylinder fuel injected engine

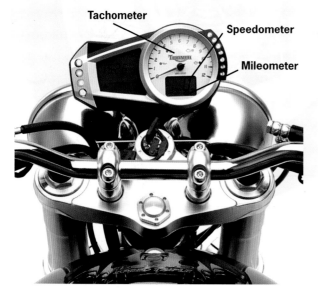

Tachometer

Speedometer

Mileometer

Clear display

The display between the handlebars gives the rider important information. The tachometer – the dial with the red needle – shows revs per minute (rpm). The speedometer on the Speed Triple is just below the needle. Its digital display tells the rider how fast the bike is going. The mileometer shows how far the bike has travelled since it was bought. The mileometer on the Speed Triple is built into the tachometer display.

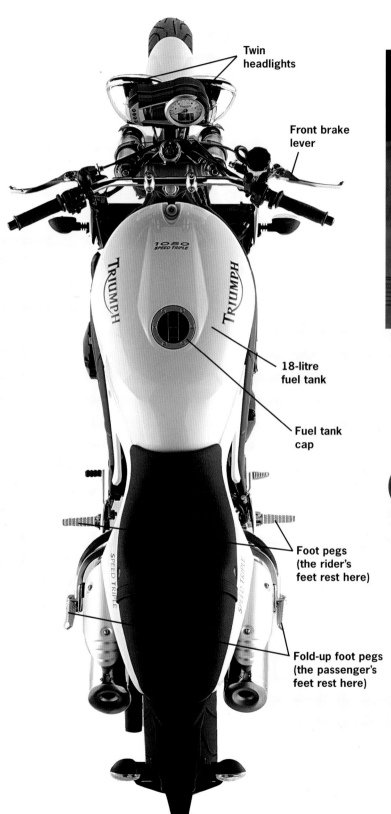

Twin
headlights

Front brake
lever

1050
SPEED TRIPLE

TRIUMPH

TRIUMPH

18-litre
fuel tank

Fuel tank
cap

SPEED TRIPLE

Foot pegs
(the rider's
feet rest here)

Fold-up foot pegs
(the passenger's
feet rest here)

Tech talk

Rpm – revs per minute: the number of times the rotating parts of the engine go round every minute.

Shock absorbers – devices that are designed to absorb forces and impacts to the suspension.

Swingarm – a moveable joint between the frame of the motorbike and the rear wheel.

HOT SPOT

Suspension

Suspension is important for a comfortable ride, keeping the seat level even when the bike is riding over rough surfaces and the wheels are juddering up and down. Springs within shock absorbers on the front forks cushion and smooth out these jarring movements, making it easier both to steer and stay on the bike.

Triumph Daytona 675

The Daytona 675 is Triumph's new middleweight racing machine. It was launched in spring 2006 and won new Triumph fans as well as several awards.

Daytona engine

The Daytona 675 has a 3-cylinder engine – a feature that sets it apart from the middleweight racing bikes produced by other companies, most of which have 4-cylinder engines. It is also slightly smaller than most of its competitors but outperforms them in almost every respect.

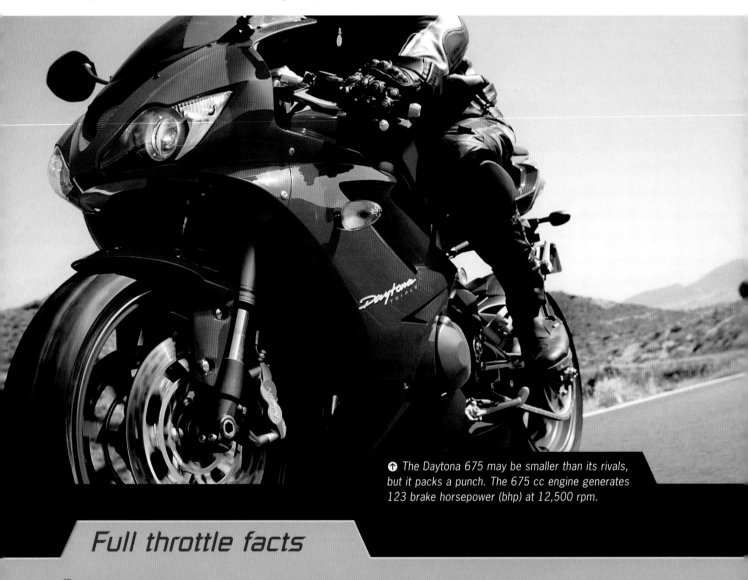

⬆ The Daytona 675 may be smaller than its rivals, but it packs a punch. The 675 cc engine generates 123 brake horsepower (bhp) at 12,500 rpm.

Full throttle facts

Top speed: 262 kph
Length: 2,010 mm

Handlebar width: 710 mm
Fuel capacity: 17.4 litres

Circuit racing

The Daytona 675 is sold for use on public roads, but it was designed and built with circuit racing in mind. Motorbike circuit racing is one of the world's most challenging and dangerous sports.
The riders take great risks as they roar around the specially made courses as fast as they can, all the time trying to stay ahead of the other bikes on the track.

⬆ The Daytona 675 comes in three colours: graphite, scorched yellow and tornado red.

Kerb weight: 165 kg
Seat height: 825 mm

Engine capacity: 675 cc
Gearbox: 6-speed

Ideal shape

The shape of the Daytona 675 is designed so the rider leans forward towards the handlebars. This lowers the rider's height on the bike and makes the rider and bike more streamlined. This means the bike can travel faster than it would if the rider was sitting up straight. The engine is unusually narrow and is shielded by a smooth, sweeping fairing. This also improves the bike's streamlining. Even the gearbox is designed to save space and weight – it is fitted vertically to make the engine shorter.

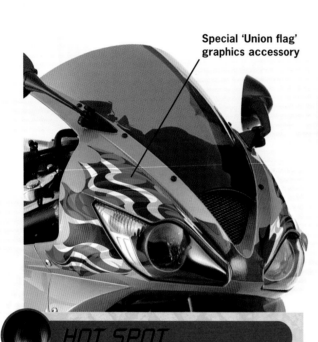

Special 'Union flag' graphics accessory

Mirrors

Under seat triple-outlet exhaust

'O'-ring drive chain

HOT SPOT

Windshield and headlights

Most racing bikes have low, sloping windshields to make them more streamlined. On the Daytona 675, the windshield is built into the front fairing and is made from polycarbonate. The two headlights are positioned just below the windshield. One headlight is dipped and the other is full-beam. Riders used dipped headlights so that they do not dazzle oncoming drivers, but full-beam lights up more of the road ahead.

↑ This rear view clearly shows how wide the rear tyre is on the Daytona 675. It has a very widely spaced tread pattern like that seen on track-racing motorbikes.

Triumph Daytona 675

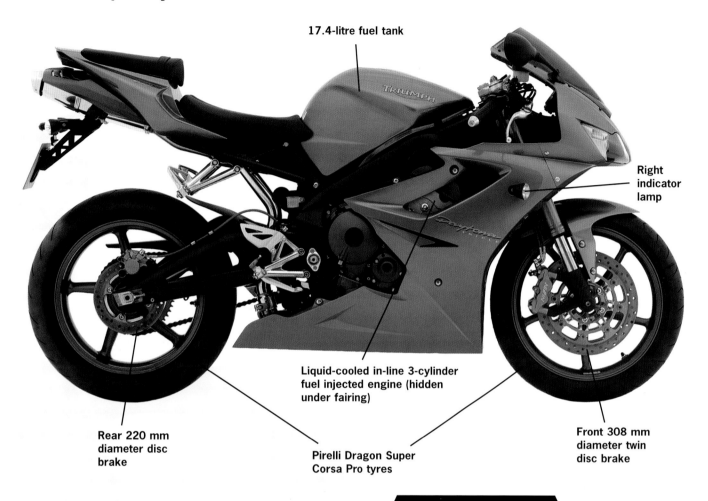

17.4-litre fuel tank

Right indicator lamp

Liquid-cooled in-line 3-cylinder fuel injected engine (hidden under fairing)

Rear 220 mm diameter disc brake

Pirelli Dragon Super Corsa Pro tyres

Front 308 mm diameter twin disc brake

Racing tyres

Motorbikes have different types of tyre for different uses and road conditions. Racing tyres have very little tread because they ride over a flat, track surface. Racing tyres become slightly sticky as they warm up, so they grip the track very well. The tyre on the back wheel, which is powered by the engine, is wider than the one on the front. This increases grip because there is more tyre in contact with the road surface as the bike powers along.

Tech talk

Fairing – a shell, usually made of plastic or fibreglass, fitted over the frame of some motorbikes to shield the rider and chassis from the wind.

Polycarbonate – a type of very strong plastic.

Streamlined – something that is shaped to pass smoothly through air.

Tread – the bumps and grooves on a tyre.

Triumph Rocket III

The Rocket III is Triumph's largest production motorbike, weighing almost twice as much as the Daytona 675. Its engine is the biggest of any production road bike in the world – at 2294 cc it is larger than most car engines.

Drive shaft

The Rocket III is a cruiser, built for comfort and effortless riding. Its huge engine delivers massive power: 140 brake horsepower (bhp) at 6,000 rpm. It is so powerful that the rear wheel is driven via a metal shaft, because a belt or a chain would not be strong enough.

⬆ The Rocket III is massive but handles well. It is a bike built for cruising on long journeys.

Full throttle facts

Top speed: 240 kph
Length: 2,500 mm

Handlebar width: 970 mm
Fuel capacity: 24 litres

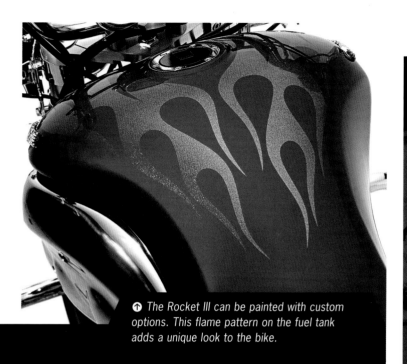

↑ The Rocket III can be painted with custom options. This flame pattern on the fuel tank adds a unique look to the bike.

Custom options

The Rocket III is designed to be customised by owners, and a huge number of accessories are available for it. These range from small details, such as heated hand grips and chrome axle nut covers, to custom paint jobs and a choice of seat styles. In total, there are almost 50 optional extras for owners to choose from.

↗ The optional back rest gives a passenger support, while the small luggage rack can be used to attach a bag to the rear of the bike.

Kerb weight: 320 kg
Seat height: 740 mm

Engine capacity: 2294 cc
Gearbox: 5-speed

Powerful and stable

The Rocket III is a bike built around an engine – the largest of any two-wheeled production machine on the road. Its pistons are as big as those of a Dodge Viper V10 muscle car; a high-performance road car produced in the USA. The Rocket III is an awesome bike, but it is one that has its weight spread evenly. The long wheelbase makes it very stable and its centre of gravity is low. This means it is easy to keep the bike upright when it stops and easy to manoeuvre at low speed.

Tech talk

Pillion seat – a seat for a passenger.

Piston – a metal rod that moves up and down inside a cylinder.

Wheelbase – the distance between the front and rear axles.

Triumph Rocket III

Digital engine management system

Detachable pillion seat

Radiator

5-spoke alloy wheel

Liquid-cooled, 2294 cc in-line 3-cylinder fuel injected engine

Slash-cut single exhaust

⬆ The Rocket III combines classic crusier styling with top performance.

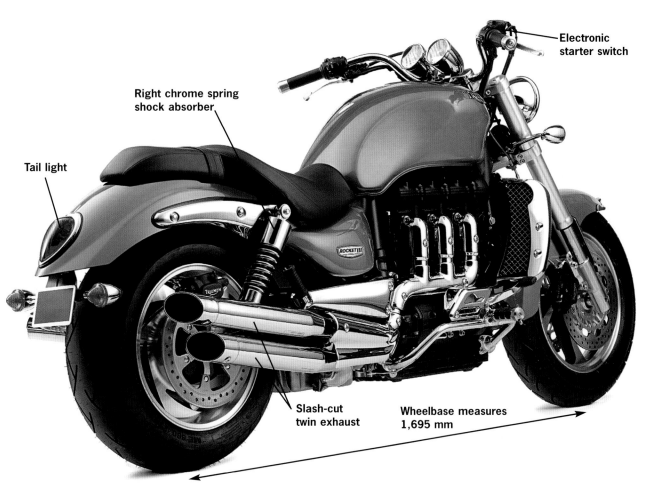

Electronic starter switch

Right chrome spring shock absorber

Tail light

Slash-cut twin exhaust

Wheelbase measures 1,695 mm

HOT SPOT

Fuel injection

Fuel-injected engines are used in many bikes to deliver high-performance. It is an electronic system that checks exactly how much fuel is sprayed into the engine cylinders to generate power. This also increases engine fuel efficiency because exactly the right amount of fuel is burned.

↑ *The Rocket III is an eye-catching machine and turns heads on any street.*

The Thruxton is a classic sports bike, inspired by the café racing machines Triumph built in the 1960s (see opposite page). It has a distinctively retro look, which sets it apart from most other bikes on the road.

Classic style, modern features

The Thruxton has the look of a bike from the 1960s, but everything else about it is modern. For example, the engine is started by a digital ignition system.

↑ The Thruxton design harks back to the 1960s 'Golden Age' and looks quite unlike most other modern motorbikes.

Full throttle facts

Top speed: 177 kph
Length: 2,150 mm

Handlebar width: 695 mm
Fuel capacity: 16.6 litres

The Thruxton is inspired by the bikes that rockers rode down to Brighton and other towns on the south coast of England in the 1960s.

Tech talk

Ignition system – the system that starts a vehicle's engine.

Mudguard – the piece of metal positioned between the forks and over the top of the wheel. It prevents mud and other debris flicking up and hitting the rider.

Retro – short for retrospective. Looking back towards or inspired by the past.

HOT SPOT

Café racers

The café racer Triumphs of the 1960s were the favoured bikes of Britain's rockers. The Thruxton has kept many of the features of those classic Triumph bikes, including the chromed, wire-spoked wheels, the swept-back handlebars, the distinctive seat hump and the shorty-style front mudguard. The two colour options are classic too: Jet Black or Tornado Red, with a bold stripe down the centre of the fuel tank.

 Kerb weight: 205 kg
Seat height: 790 mm

Engine capacity: 865 cc
Gearbox: 5-speed

Thruxton vs Triton

The Thruxton was launched in 2004.
It owes a lot, in terms of its styling,
to the Triton – one of the original café
racing bikes first seen in the late 1950s.
The Triton was a combination of parts
from two different bike manufacturers,
Triumph and Norton, and the two
names gave birth to the 'Tri-ton'.
The Thruxton has the Triton's short,
'clip-on' handlebars and a large,
single headlight. Its engine is
also a parallel-twin – an engine
with two cylinders, which line up
together. However, the Thruxton's
engine is larger and more advanced
than the ones in the Triton bikes.

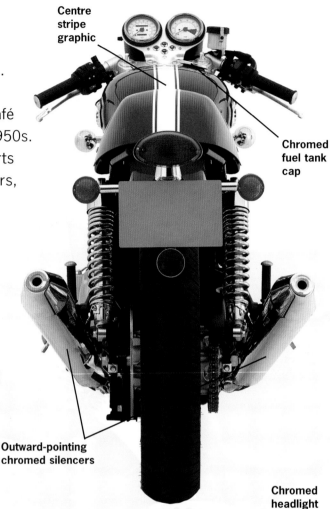

Centre
stripe
graphic

Chromed
fuel tank
cap

Outward-pointing
chromed silencers

Triumph Thruxton

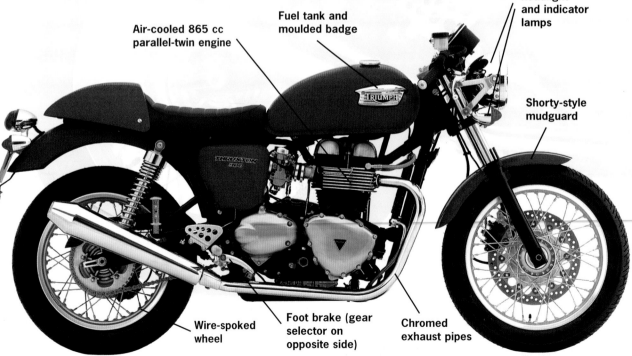

Air-cooled 865 cc
parallel-twin engine

Fuel tank and
moulded badge

Chromed
headlight
and indicator
lamps

Shorty-style
mudguard

Wire-spoked
wheel

Foot brake (gear
selector on
opposite side)

Chromed
exhaust pipes

Short handlebars

The Thruxton's handlebars are short and swept backwards, which means that the rider's hands are positioned closely together. The left handgrip is fixed and does not move. The right hand controls the throttle. By twisting the handgrip, the rider can rev the engine and make the bike accelerate when in gear. Gears are selected by foot using a lever on the left-hand side of the engine. Between the handlebars are two dials – the speedometer on the left and the tachometer on the right.

Tech talk

Silencer – an attachment on the end of a motorcycle's exhaust pipe, which makes the bike quieter than it would otherwise be.

Speedometer – an instrument that displays the speed at which the bike is travelling.

Tachometer – an instrument that displays the number of engine revolutions per minute (rpm).

Throttle – a device that controls the flow of fuel to an engine – the faster the flow, the higher the speed.

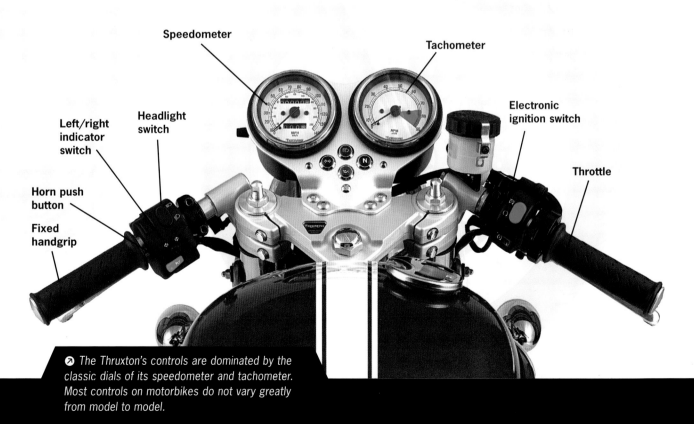

Speedometer

Tachometer

Left/right indicator switch

Headlight switch

Electronic ignition switch

Horn push button

Throttle

Fixed handgrip

⊘ *The Thruxton's controls are dominated by the classic dials of its speedometer and tachometer. Most controls on motorbikes do not vary greatly from model to model.*

Triumph America

The name of this bike gives a big clue to the place that inspired it. At first sight, the America could be mistaken for a big machine from the USA, but its heart is all British. The design is based on another bike produced by Triumph – the Bonneville.

⬆ The Triumph America brings together classic British engineering with cruiser styling, and is a relaxed and easy bike to ride.

Full throttle facts

Top speed: 169 kph
Length: 2,420 mm

Handlebar width: 960 mm
Fuel capacity: 16.6 litres

Brakes

The Triumph America's brakes are like those fitted to most motorbikes. It has disc brakes on both the front and rear wheels. When the rider applies the front brake with his or her right hand, pads are forced against the metal discs and the front wheel slows down. The back wheel is controlled separately with a foot brake.

Great cruising

The America is a cruiser, built for comfortable riding over long distances. It has wide handlebars, a low, comfortable seat and forward-set 'highway pegs' which act as foot rests on long journeys. Its engine is very responsive. A slow twist of the throttle gives great acceleration without even needing to change gear. This makes overtaking both safer and easier, because it allows the rider to focus all of his or her concentration on the road ahead.

⊘ *The Triumph America is a well-balanced bike for both rider and pillion passenger.*

Kerb weight: 226 kg
Seat height: 720 mm

Engine capacity: 865 cc
Gearbox: 5-speed

Triumph America

Tank-mounted warning lights

16.6 litre fuel tank

Forward-set foot pegs (left and right) for upright seating position

Chromed cone-shaped silencers

Comfort zone

Sitting on the Triumph America is almost like sitting in your favourite armchair. The seat is wide, soft and padded to give a comfortable ride no matter how long the journey. It is also set quite low down so that the rider can easily put both feet flat on the ground when the bike is stopped.

Cruiser chrome

Chrome is a silver-coloured metal widely used on motorbikes, particularly cruisers like the America. It is chosen for its attractive appearance and can be highly polished to give a perfect, mirror-like shine.

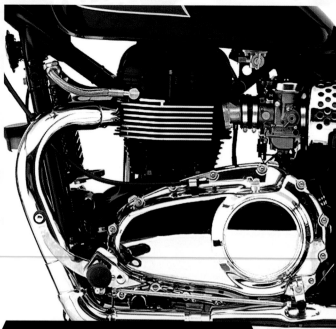

⊕ *Many bikes have chrome details to really catch the eye out on the road.*

Fuel efficient

The America's 865 cc engine is large enough to provide plenty of power even with a pillion passenger. It is also very fuel efficient, generating around 42 mpg, making it relatively cheap to run and perfect for long trips.

Wide handlebars
(960 mm)

Air intakes
(left and
right)

Wide, 41 mm
'telescopic'
front fork

Front 310 mm
disc brake

865 cc, air-cooled,
twin carburettor
engine

Rear 285 mm
disc brake

Triumph Sprint ST

The Triumph Sprint ST combines comfort and top performance, and is designed to appeal to a wide range of riders.

Sports tourer

The letters ST stand for sports tourer, which means that this bike offers something for both sports and touring bike riders. The current model has a sporty 1050 cc, fuel-injected engine balanced with a tourer body that includes colour co-ordinated panniers.

⬆ The Triumph Sprint ST is the perfect combination of sports and touring styles – it's like a work of art.

Full throttle facts

Top speed: 259 kph
Length: 2,114 mm

Handlebar width: 750 mm
Fuel capacity: 20 litres

Tech talk

Fuel-injection – a device that forces fuel directly into an engine producing rapid acceleration.

Panniers – storage bins or boxes made to fit on the sides of a bike.

HOT SPOT

ABS

The Sprint ST is fitted with an optional ABS – an anti-lock braking system – still an unusual feature on most motorbikes. ABS makes it safer to stop suddenly, even when the brakes are slammed on hard. The wheels never completely lock up when the brakes are applied, so the rider is less likely to skid and fall off the bike.

⬆ *Although the Sprint ST is very comfortable, it can be ridden like a sports bike too.*

Kerb weight: 210 kg
Seat height: 805 mm

Engine capacity: 1050 cc
Gearbox: 6-speed

Mapping the way

The instrumentation on this bike is state-of-the-art and includes an LCD trip computer, which calculates journey information. Optional extras include a global positioning system (GPS). The GPS uses satellite technology to tell the rider exactly where he or she is.

↑ This is the LCD trip computer that displays travel information to the rider.

Tech talk

Indicators – orange flashing lights, which tell other road users you are going to turn left or right.

LCD – liquid crystal display; a type of screen (many flat-screen TVs now have LCD).

Triple exhaust outlet under seat

Liquid-cooled, 1050 cc in-line 3-cylinder fuel injected engine

Air duct to help cool the engine

Disc brake fluid

Indicator lamps mounted in the mirrors

Triple front headlight

Optional ABS (anti-lock braking system)

Triumph Sprint ST

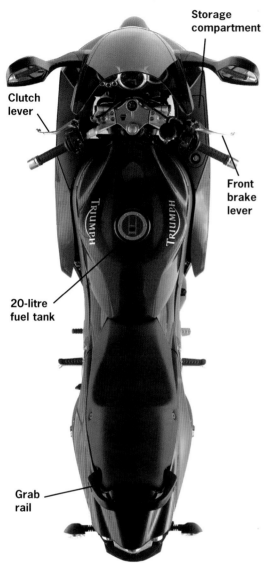

Storage compartment

Clutch lever

Front brake lever

20-litre fuel tank

Grab rail

Large capacity

A bike built for travelling at speed over long distances needs a large fuel tank, otherwise the rider would have to stop often to refuel. The Sprint ST is well equipped – its fuel tank has a capacity of 20 litres. The bike also comes fitted with two panniers (see page 26) that fit neatly onto the back.

⬆ *The Sprint ST's fuel-injected engine generates 123 bhp.*

It takes two

The Triumph ST is designed to take a passenger. The pillion seat is built in, not removable as it is on some other bikes. Just behind the pillion seat is a grab rail. This gives passengers something to hold on to, other than the rider's waist. This is important, as it reduces the chances of them falling off the back of the bike when it accelerates.

Glossary

Alloy – a mixture of different metals.

Brake horsepower (bhp) – the amount of power generated by an engine that is actually used and transferred to the wheels.

Café racers – the home-modified bikes ridden in the 1950s and 1960s. Their riders met up at venues, such as the Ace Café in London, which inspired the name.

Carburettor – a device that mixes fuel with air before it is forced into an engine.

cc – short for cubic centimetres, it is used as a measurement of the size of the engine's cylinders.

Chassis – the basic frame of a motorbike to which all other components are attached.

Cruiser – a motorbike usually with a small petrol tank, an upright riding style and feet-forward seating.

Cylinders – the places in an engine where fuel and air are ignited to generate power.

Drive chain – similar to a bicycle chain, it is a chain that transfers power from the engine to the rear wheel.

Drive shaft – a metal rod or shaft that transfers power from the engine to the rear wheel.

Handling – how a motorbike responds when being ridden, such as how it turns into and out of corners.

Horsepower (hp) – a unit of measurement used to describe the amount of power an engine generates.

Pillion – the back seat on a motorbike for its passenger.

Rocker – a style of dress and behaviour from the 1960s. Rockers had slicked back hair, wore leather and rode around on motorbikes in gangs.

rpm – short for revolutions per minute; a measurement of the speed of a motorbike's engine.

Satellite – an object circling the Earth. Man-made satellites are used to transmit information to global positioning systems (GPS), used on some bikes.

Shock absorbers – devices which are designed to absorb sudden forces and impacts to the suspension of the vehicle.

Suspension – the system of springs, shock absorbers and other components, directly connected to the wheels or the axles that affects the handling of a vehicle.

Swing arm – a moveable joint between the frame of the motorbike and the rear wheel assembly.

Tachometer – a dial or display that tells the rider the speed of the engine in revolutions per minute (rpm).

Wheelbase – the distance between the front and rear axles of motorbike.

Further information

Websites

http://www.triumph.co.uk/

The official Triumph website. It has detailed information and pictures of all the models in the company's current range of motorbikes.

http://www.bikez.com/brand/triumph.php

A list of all Triumph bikes produced since 1970, with links to other pages filled with detailed information.

http://www.ianchadwick.com/motorcycles/triumph/

A huge site packed with facts about Triumph's history.

http://www.tomcc.org/

The official site of the Triumph Owners Motor Cycle Club.

Books

Triumph Motorcycles: Their Renaissance and the Hinckley Factory

Johnny Tipler (The Crowood Press, 2006).
The story of how Triumph came back from the brink, illustrated with lots of photographs.

The Triumph Story

David Minton (Haynes Group, 2003).
A detailed look at the history of Triumph racing and production motorcycles, from 1902 to the present day.

Triumph Motorcycles: A Century of Passion and Power

Lindsay Brooke (Motorbooks International, 2002).
An in-depth account of the ups and downs of the Triumph company, together with the bikes it produces.

Triumph timeline

1883 – Siegfried Bettmann, a German immigrant, sets up the S. Bettmann Import Export Agency in London and sells bicycles.

1886 – Bettmann changes the name of his company to Triumph Cycle Company, but it's not registered officially until 1887.

1902 – Triumph produces its first motorbike in Coventry, which uses an imported Belgian engine.

1905 – Triumph builds its first completely British motorbike, using only British labour and parts.

1907 – Triumph bikes place second and third in the first ever Isle Of Man TT race.

1939-45 – The British government takes many Triumph bikes for military use.

1950 – The Thunderbird, one of Triumph's all-time classic bikes, is launched.

1958 – Triumph launches the Bonneville. It is hailed as the greatest motorbike ever made.

1969 – Triumph production peaks with almost 48,000 motorbikes built in one year.

1972 – Triumph becomes one third of Norton-Villiers-Triumph as sales start to crash.

1973 – The Triumph plant closes down.

1974 – A new company, Meriden Motorcycle Cooperative, is created with government help and the Triumph plant reopens.

1983 – Triumph goes bankrupt and the brand is bought by Mr John Bloor.

1990 – Mr Bloor opens the new production plant at Hinckley and unveils new Triumph models.

1994 – The Speed Triple is launched.

1995 – Triumph USA is set up to distribute Triumph motorbikes in the United States.

1999 – Triumph launches the Sprint ST.

2003 – The first Triumph America goes on sale.

2004 – The Thruxton and Rocket III are launched.

2006 – The Daytona 675 is launched to critical acclaim. The model is sold out through pre-orders before production even begins.

Index